15 Essential CICHLID
Fish Facts That You May Have Never Known

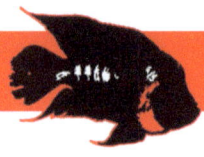

Copyright 2018 © Lawrence E. Smith
Skip's Aquarium Maintenance Service LLC

All rights reserved.

This publication is designed to provide competent and reliable inspirational information regarding subject matter covered. No part of this publication may be reproduced, stored in a retrieval system, or transmitted, in any form or by any means, electronic, mechanical, photocopying, recording, or otherwise, without the prior written permission of the author, except for brief quotes used in review.

Publishing Company
Skip's Aquarium Maintenance Service LLC

Graphic Designer
William Harris of Cre8tive Conceptions

Sensory modalities in cichlid fish behavior chart author
Elsevier

Editor and Chief
Sonya Smith

Freelance Editor
Jamal Bailey

Skip's Website: www.realhardcichlids.com
Publication Date: April 2018
Imprint:
Skip's Aquarium Maintenance Service LLC
ISBN-978-0-9836603-1-6
Made in USA

ABOUT THE AUTHOR

Skip A.K.A. fishlaw1 grew up as the only child in Washington, D.C. and was introduced to the wonderful world of all things aquatic before his father died. He was further exposed to tropical fish by his uncles on both sides of his family. His uncle "June" and late uncle Sterling heavily influenced him into keeping fish. Also, his mother nurtured his passion and love of fish. Skip has always felt he was born into the fish hobby and not introduced. Now fast forward to present date Skip has turned that passion into a successful business involving tropical fish. He has created his own Cichlid bloodline and certified certificates. Also, he has authored and self-published his own book titled **"Skip's Guide to Keeping Real Hard Cichlids"** currently on Amazon. After years of researching information for his first book, he has become obsessed with fish and aquatic information, which has led to him to writing second book.

II.

III.

ABOUT THE AUTHOR

15

Essential Cichlid Fish Facts That You May Have Never Known

This Book is dedicated to all my Facebook followers and YouTube Subscribers who have joined me in my journey through this great Aquatic Community.

Introduction - When it comes to raising and breeding cichlids, finding any books that accurately reference and detail this process is scarce and very limited. The idea of creating a guide and manual that will spark conversation, motivate and engage the fish-keeping community serves as my purpose to write this book. This manual will serve as an accurate and detailed reference guide to help both old and new aquatic hobbyist and cichlid keepers.

My parents and extended relatives exposed me to the world of raising and keeping both tropical and non-tropical fish as early as age five. One of my fondest memories was receiving a five- gallon fish tank set-up by my mom, which included a fish we named "Big Fish". That experience was the leading catalyst to the creation of Skip's Aquarium Maintenance Services, LLC and Real Hard Cichlids Aquatic Kennels. Since, then I have always had a passion to study all things fish and aquatics. I hope this book will educate and inspire all who love this hobby.

Happy Reading!!!

What is a Cichlid?

Before detailing some of the most important facts you need to know when keeping cichlids, research the true definition of what a cichlid is. *Cichlids are fish from the family Cichlidae in the order Perciformes.* They are members of a suborder known as Labroidei, along with the wrasses (Labridae), damselfishes (Pomacentridae), and surf perches (Embiotocidae). This family is both large and diverse with over 1,600 species having been scientifically described making it one of the largest vertebrate families. New species are discovered annually with many species remaining undescribed.

Most cichlids originate from Africa and Central / South America. The actual number of species is unknown, with estimates varying between 2,000 and 3,000. Their personalities make them a popular freshwater fish often kept in home aquariums. Some of the larger more aggressive cichlids love to "glass-bang" while chasing their owner's hands around the tank. This being an effective way for fish hobbyist to interact with their "wet-pet".

v.

FOREWORD

The creative force of the aquatic universe led me on the path to new discoveries in this hobby. This motivated me to define my present and future in terms of my history in this Aquatic community. Along the way the burden of knowledge sometimes grew heavy and I had to stop for a while and review my purpose. I wanted to inject my experience, thoughts and feelings from my journey and that is why I started **Skip Smith Facebook Page** and **Fishlaw1 YouTube Channel**. The goal is to keep my Facebook and YouTube followers informed about the changes that occur with the cichlids we all love. At **Real Hard Cichlids Aquatic Kennels** we focus on the developement of healthy fish by selective breeding, striving for a well rounded end result by constantly eliminating unwanted charateristics. Our motto is to provide knowledge and great customer service, which results in healthy business relationships.

TABLE OF CONTENTS

FACT #1
Cichlids are one of the largest vertebrate families in the world

FACT #2
Most cichlids are secondary freshwater fish

FACT #3
Large healthy cichlids can go 7-10 days without eating

FACT #4
The average life-span of Cichlids

FACT #5
Some cichlids can live in saltwater.

FACT #6
Cichlids are not only located in Africa, Central and South America

FACT #7
Most cichlid species are Omnivorous

FACT #8
Some cichlids can feed their young using skin secretion from their mucous gland

FACT #9
Cichlids are the fastest growing evolution of all vertebrates

FACT #10
Cichlids are used worldwide to study evolution

FACT #11
Cichlids sleep with their eyes open

FACT #12
Cichlids can hear

FACT #13
Harmful natural enemies of cichlids

FACT #14
Cichlids are protective and nurturing parents

FACT #15
Cichlids can adapt faster and better than any species of fish.

FACT #1

Cichlids are one of the largest vertebrate families in the world.

They are most diverse in Africa and South America. The continent of Africa alone is estimated to host at least 1,600 cichlid species. Central America and Mexico are estimated to hold roughly 120 species reaching as far north as the Rio Grande located in southern Texas. Asia is known to host but a few different species of cichlids. Now we cannot talk about what is a cichlid without discussing what's not a cichlid. All cichlids are freshwater fish, although, a few are occasionally found in brackish water and rarely in coastal marine areas. There are many marine and fresh water fish that resembles cichlids, but after careful observation that are revealed not to be. Let's keep in mind that the Cichlidae is just one of 482 families of fish. There are over 25,000 species of fish all together, which incidentally is more than all the birds, mammals, reptiles and amphibians combined. Would you believe that the beloved "Alligator gar" and "Large Mouth Bass", are freshwater predators, but not cichlids? And the marine fish "Queen Angel" fits into this category.

Evolutionary Relationships

How do cichlids fit into the 25,000 species of living fish? In a nutshell, living fish can be in 5 different classes. The largest of which is called Actinopterygii or boney-finned fish. Other classes include: hagfish (Class Myxini) and sharks (Class Chondichthyes). Humans and all other land vertebrates are fish falling in to (Class Sarcopterygii or lobe-finned fish and it should be *noted that we do not include the number of land vertebrates in the count of the fish. There are 57 orders of fish and 42 of these are Actinopterygians. These include: sturgeons, gars, eels, herrings, minnows, catfish, pike, smelt, perch-like and this list goes on. This is a huge group of organisms comprising over 23,000 species. Within this bounty of diversity there is one order that has exceeded all others in generating new and different forms and this is the order Perciformes or referred to as perch-like fish.

FACT #1 cont.

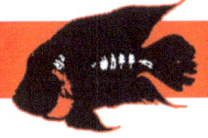

The Perciform fish (order #55 according to Nelson 1994) contains 148 families in almost 1500 genera, encompassing almost 10,000 species.

One of those families is the Cichlidae. The cichlids make up a disproportionate number of the Perciform fish ranking second in number only to the gobies (Gobiidae). Other large families of perciform fish include the wrasses (Labridae), sea basses (Serranidae), blennies (Blenniidae), damselfish (Pomacentridae), drums and croakers (Sciaenidae) and cardinalfish (Apogonidae) all of which have more than 200 species a piece.

Ichthyologists do not fully understand all the complex relationships within the Perciformes; however, it seems relatively certain that the Cichlidae belong in a cluster of closely related families. These families include wrasses (Labridae), the damselfishes (Pomacentridae) and the surfperches (Embiotocidae). This cluster is called the Suborder Labridae: A Clownfish; Pomacentridae is in the "Suborder Labroidei" also the Wrasses: Labridae and cichlid Cichlidae.

FACT #2

Most cichlids are secondary freshwater fish meaning that they derived from seawater fish that again populated the freshwater.

This gives them a great advantage over other species whose ancestors never went back to the sea, because they have a much higher tolerance for salt than primary freshwater fish. This allows them to colonize in waters that are high in dissolved minerals.

It is believed that the first cichlids may have inhabited the rivers of Africa, where we still find some species today. Many years ago, the Great African Rift cut through the Congo River the inflowing of what is today the Malaragasi River and forming Lake Tanganyika. The water became stagnant and was warmed by the sun; as well as, geothermal energy exposed at the bottom of the Rift. At the same time, large quantities of salts were dissolved from the underlying exposed rocky lake floor making it difficult for primary fresh water fish to colonize the new lake. However, for cichlids this newly formed environment became a dream pool rich in nutrients and food and low in competition.

Lake Tanganyika is the largest museum of natural history in the world and often regarded as the oldest isolated body of water cichlids could settle. Geological studies have revealed that Lake Tanganyika is at least 20 million years old and its water level is known to rise and drop repeatedly. This caused the lake to split into two or even three separate lakes for a long period of time before combining again into one lake.

FACT #3

Large healthy cichlids can go 7-10 days without eating (depending on the species involved).

Cichlids surprisingly can fast, but exactly how long is dependent on several factors. Such as how large the fish is, how old it is, and whether it is a carnivore or herbivore. Exceptions can be found, but generally, large or older fish can go without fish food longer than small or young fish. It's pretty much a straightforward case of reserves. Large or older fish simply have more body mass and fat reserves they can draw upon. Thus, for example, a Jack Dempsey cichlid can go significantly longer without fish food than a Black Nasty (haitiensis). However, aquariums containing baby fish should be fed after a day or two.

My own experience proving this fact was when I went on vacation for a week without feeding my adult cichlids and they were fine upon my return home. However, I did suffer some losses among my fry. Be sure that you are mindful of your fish maturity when determining feeding duration.

FACT #4

**The average life-span of most aquarium raised cichlids is between 10-15 years
(may vary depending on size and species).
Cichlids in the wild can survive between 5 - 60 years
(depending on the species).**

RED ISLETAS

Please note, this is a very broad statement considering the many different types of cichlids. Maintaining good water quality and avoiding overfeeding increases cichlid life-span and keeps sickness and diseases to a minimum or non-existing.

FACT #5

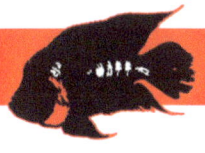

Some cichlids can live in saltwater.

When performing water changes to my own aquariums I routinely add salt, but not enough to register on a gravity meter. In fact, salt is known to prevent infection in wounded cichlids. There are many species of African cichlids that tolerate brackish water, but cannot withstand straight saltwater; however, a few can, but not many. Cichlids have long been known to be euryhaline - tolerant of a wide range in salinity.

While some new world cichlids can endure salty water, others live in isolated inland lakes where water has evaporated over thousands of years leaving minerals behind; resulting in lakes with high ion concentrations.

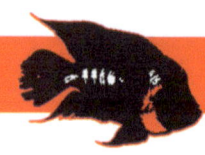

FACT #5 cont.

There are also Central and South American cichlid species that can live in saltwater such as the "Mayan" (Cichlasoma Urophthalmus) and the "Black Belt" (Vieja maculicauda) cichlids, which can regularly be found in the ocean. Much research has been performed on salinity tolerance in the Mayan cichlid due to its potential as a food fish. Despite the tolerance to saltwater of the black belt cichlid and Mayan cichlid some species are not so flexible and are stenohaline.

They are only able to tolerate a narrow range of salinity. Experimental evidence and literature shows that many species of Central American cichlids can withstand wide ranges of salinity. Some appear to be unaffected by low salt concentrations (ex: convict, redhead),

FACT #5 cont.

others prefer brackish water to freshwater (ex: Mayan, Jack Dempsey). While full strength sea water may be too strong for some species if not given enough time to acclimate (ex: Mayan, red devil, blackbelt), it is possible for others to make a complete transition if given enough time (Mayan, black belt).

Knowledge of salinity tolerance and salinity preference could allow new captive species combinations and provide ideal artificial conditions for your cichlid.

FACT #6

Contrary to popular belief, cichlids are not only located in Africa, Central and South America,

GREAT LAKES...

FACT #6 cont.

... but also found in Asia,
the Middle East and Australia.

...OF THE WORLD

FACT #6 cont.

Although, you may be able to find beautiful cichlids in aquariums across the world, there are only a limited number of geographical locations a cichlid would call home. A few species are found as far north as Texas here in the United States and as far South as Argentina. Also, cichlids can be found in certain areas of the Middle East in waters surrounding Sri Lanka, Madagascar and off the southern coast of India with a few species endemic to Asia. There are nine species of Asian cichlids which can be found in Lebanon, Israel, Syria, Iran, India and Sri Lanka.

Species List:
- Astatotilapia flaviijosephi
- Paretrophus Maculatus
- Mango Tilapia
- Redbelly Tilapia
- Tristramella Sacra
- Tristramella Simonsis
- Canara Pearlspot
- Green Chromide
- Iranocichla Hormuzensis

Two or three species, belonging to the genus Etroplus, are fond on the Asian Continent.

With so many different species, the cichlid family is a lesson in diversity. Knowing the true origins of where your cichlid is from gives you a better understanding of their requirements and ideal conditions for successful fish-keeping.

FACT #7

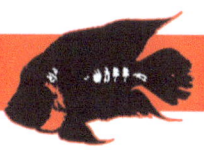

Most cichlid species are Omnivorous

With such a wide variety of different cichlid species, the feeding habits may vary. However, most cichlids have an enormous appetite and are easily fed. Examples of omnivorous cichlids include: Cichlasomines, Angelfish, many

West African species and Heros species. In the wild, these fish feed mostly on insects, crustaceans, worms and sometimes also eating plants. In aquariums these species should be fed a mixed diet of live foods, flake foods, and plant or vegetable matter.

FACT #7 cont

Carnivorous Cichlids
(predatory species specializing in eating other fish)

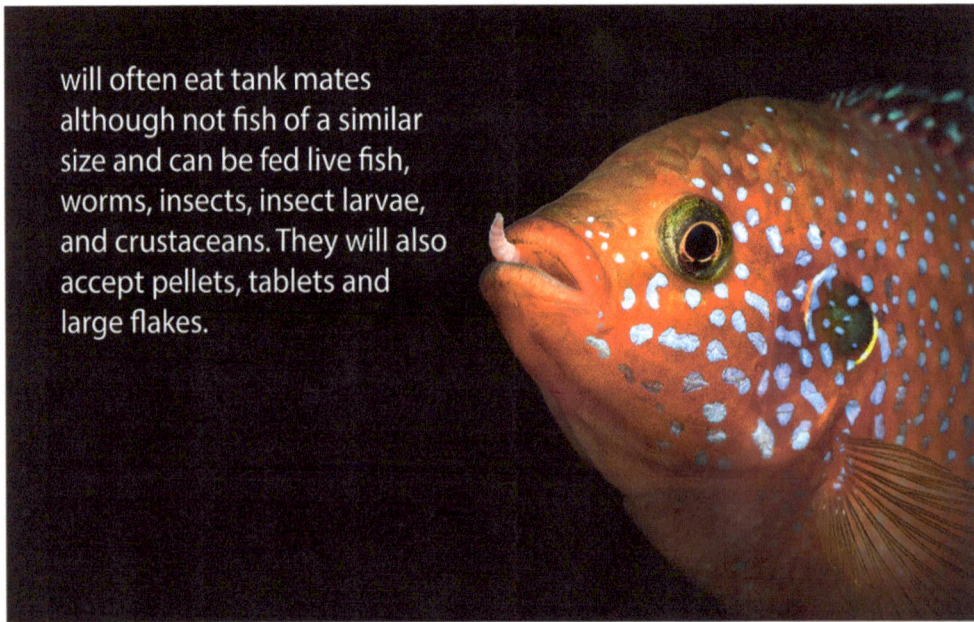

will often eat tank mates although not fish of a similar size and can be fed live fish, worms, insects, insect larvae, and crustaceans. They will also accept pellets, tablets and large flakes.

FACT #7 cont

Herbivorous Cichlids
(species that prefer to feed on plant matter).

 These fish will eat live aquarium plants. In aquariums, herbivorous cichlids feed on plant-based flakes, pellet foods, plants, and vegetables. Some herbivorous species (ex: Lake Malawi Mbunas, Lake Tanganyika Tropheus) feed on micro-organisms and crustaceans (known as Aufwuchs) commonly embedded deep in thick algae that grows on rocks.

FACT #8

Some cichlids can feed their young using skin secretion from their mucous gland.

Cells which are specialized to secrete mucus are called mucous cells. Examples in the GI include secretory cells of the salivary glands, esophageal glands, stomach surface, pyloric glands, and Brunner's glands of the duodenum. These cells are typically organized into tubular secretory unit. Amphilophus species,

Etroplus, and Uaru species all feed their young with a skin secretion from mucous glands. Fry of the (Neolamprologus brichardi) "Fairy Cichlid", which live in large groups, are protected by adults and feed their young with a skin secretion rich in protein and produced by both parents.

FACT #9

Cichlids are the fastest growing evolution of all vertebrates.

Cichlids have evolved faster than any other vertebrate. Single species of cichlid have now evolved into 500 new species during a period of a million years, while in comparison, the ape has only evolved into three new species after a period of 10 million years. African cichlid fish are some of the most diverse organisms on the planet with more than 2,000 known species.

Some African lakes are home to hundreds of distinct species that evolved from common ancestral species of the Nile River. Take for instance Darwin Finches, the cichlids are a dramatic example of adaptive radiation, the process by which multiple species radiate from an ancestral species through adaptation.

FACT #9 cont

I was amazed by this article online in the Stanford News and I quote "an international team of scientists, including Stanford biologists who study these cichlids fish, has sequenced the genomes of five of these species. This provides a unique insight into the genetic drivers of diversification and adaptation in all vertebrates." Other interesting facts revealed by the article is that some fish have adapted to eat the scales of other fish (Wow)!

FACT #9 cont

While others have adaptations that allow them to live among rocks and eat prey, shells included as well as, reproducing in turbulent waters carrying fertilized eggs in their mouths until they hatch.

Lastly, the article concluded that these cichlids along with Central and South American species have an enormous ability to adapt.

FACT #10

Cichlids are used worldwide to study evolution.

Researchers from the University of Wyoming have discovered more than 700 species of fish which evolved in East Africa's Lake Victoria region over the past 150,000 years. Catherine Wagner, assistant professor in the Department of Botany and the Biodiversity Institute at the University of Wyoming describes the phenomenon unparallel in the animal and plant world to be "one of the most spectacular examples of the evolution of modern biodiversity." Her research demonstrated for the first time that the rapid evolution of Lake Victoria cichlids was facilitated by earlier hybridization between distantly related cichlid species from the Upper Nile and Congo drainage systems. Wagner notes, the rapid evolution of the East African cichlids had puzzled researchers, who didn't understand how a single common ancestor could divide into 700 species so quickly. The discovery that the ancestor of these fish species was a mixture of two different ancestors from different parts of Africa, which makes it much easier to understand how the immense variety of fish in this region have evolved.

FACT #10 cont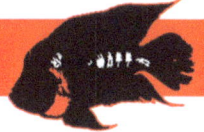

The hybridization event is estimated to have taken place around 150,000 years ago during a wet period. A Congolese lineage colonized the Lake Victoria region and encountered representatives of the Upper Nile lineage. Across the large lakes of this region, the hybrid population diversified in a process known as adaptive radiation or evolution of multiple new species adapted to different ecological niches.

While the precise course of events in ancestral Lake Victoria has yet to be reconstructed, after a dry period it filled up again about 15,000 years ago. Descendants of the genetically diverse hybrid population colonized the lake. And within the evolutionarily short period of several thousand years diverged to form at least 500 new cichlid species, with a wide variety of ecological specializations. The genetic diversity and adaptive capacity of Lake Victoria's cichlids is demonstrated by the fact that more than 40 other fish species, which colonized the lake at the same time have barely changed since then.

FACT #11

Yes! Cichlids do sleep with their eyes open.

In my own observation, I've noticed that cichlids seem to cluster together around rocks lying motionless. This unusual activity normally indicates that they are sleeping. Fish will also adopt their brightly colored "fight colors" while sleeping and often position themselves vertically. Without eyelids, it is difficult to determine when they are sleeping. They also appear sluggish and torpid for a few minutes after waking. Also, I notice when I turn on the light in my aquarium shed my fish respond erratically; almost as if they are in as trance like state. I believe this occurs because they have no eyelids, so they cannot shut their eyes completely. I would advise to turn on a non-direct light slowly to give their eyes time to adjust. This method will assure that your light will not cause any harm or life- threatening injuries.

FACT #12

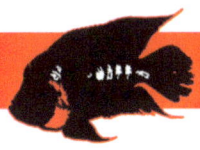

Cichlids can hear

Although we are not used to thinking of cichlids as having a well-developed sense of hearing, some fish can distinguish vibrations that are sent through the water. In fact, hearing is a rather indirect process in fish compared to mammals, which have a specialized hearing organ "ears". So, putting your home aquarium next to speakers / television or running the vacuum cleaner nearby may not be the best choice for aquarium tank placement. According to an article in Tropical Fish Magazine by Dr. Phillip Lobel recently reviewed the relatively scant literature on this topic (20001. "Acoustic Behavior of Cichlid Fishes." Journal of Aquaculture and Aquatic Sciences 9: 167-186). Lobel believes the mechanism of sound production in cichlids involves the jaw apparatus, with sounds amplified by the swimbladder. Indeed, a variety of sounds have been recorded from a number of cichlid species including Haplochromis burtoni (African riverine mouth-brooder), Hemichromic bimaculatus (African jewelfish), Herotilapia multispinosa (rainbow cichlid, Central America), Oreochromic mossambicus (Mozambique mouthbrooder), Simochromis babaulti and S. diagramma (Lake Tanganyika), and Copadichromis conophoros and Tramitichromis intermedius (Lake Malawi). In a more recent article by Amorim and associates (Amorim, M.M. Knight, Y. Stratoudakis, and G. Turner, 2004.

FACT #12 cont

"Differences in sounds made by Courting Males of Three Closely Related Lake MalawiCichlid Species." Journal of Fish Biology 65: 1358-1371) sounds from three Malawi mbuna are recorded and analyzed and the results suggest that sound may play a larger role in cichlid species recognition than we thought. In this study, three closely related species of Pseudotropheus(now Maylandia)zebra complex were studied with regard to their courtship sounds. The three species were M. Zebra, M. callaninos and M. sp. "zebra gold," which differ strikingly in male courtship colors, but are very similar in other morphological traits. As described by Amorim et al., M. Zebra are pale blue with black vertical bars, males of the undescribed species M. sp. "zebra gold" have a similar pattern of brown bars on a yellow background, while M. callainos males are uniformly pale blue. The corresponding females of M. zebra and M. sp. "zebra gold" are very similar and easily confused whereas M. callainos females are distinctively colored (blue or white). Previous genetic studies using microsatellite DNA markers show that these three species are reproductively isolated and that they mate assortative (do not hybridize in a choice situation) in the laboratory.

FACT #12 cont

Thus, they are good genetically differentiated species. Three test aquaria (5x11/2 X 2 feet), one per species, each divided into three approximately 20-inch-long compartments by two opaque, removable partitions, were used to test sound productions. Seven or eight females of the tested species were maintained in the central compartment. Each end compartment held a single male and contained a clay pot as a refuge and spawning site. Males were introduced into the end compartments and visually isolated from the females in the middle until acclimatized, typically at least 24 hours. The opaque partition was then removed and any sounds each male made recorded with a sensitive hydrophone while their behaviors could be pared. According to Amorim et al., male courtship behavior in all three species consists of a series of invariant movement/components that are not always displayed in a fixed order. These include "quiver" (male trembling in front of female); "dart" (male makes exaggerated but rapid 180-degree turns displaying opposite flanks in quick succession); "lead swim" (male flutters caudal and dorsal fins and attempts to lead female to the spawning site); "circle" (head to tail following in tight circles over the spawning site often culminating in spawning).

FACT #12 cont

The recorded sounds were made up of repeated pulses which were futher analyzed by digitization/computer sonograms oscillograms (waveform displays) into five components: sound duration; time elapsed from the start of first pulse duration; and peak frequency. Differences among species in these five sound components were tested statistically, as were differences between individual males within a species. A total of 638 sounds were successfully recorded: 212 from 11 M. sp. "zebra gold." 152 from 7 M. zebra, and 274 from 10 M. callainos males. Twelve males neither attempted courtship nor produced any sound. Sound was produced by every male that attempted to court a female. The sounds emitted by the males of these species had peak frequencies < 720 Hz, pulse durations of 9 to 12 milliseconds, a pulse period of 60 to 70 milliseconds, and sound duration varying between 500 to 700 milliseconds. To the untrained eye (mine) the sonograms and oscillograms do look slightly different, but in general are low frequency pulsed sounds and compare well with t hose from the other African cichlids already in the published literature (as above).

FACT #12 cont

Courtship behavior and sound production were significantly related with the majority of sounds being produced during the male "quiver" and "circling" displays. None of the five sound components differed significantly differences among species in pulse duration and peak frequency. Maylandia callanios was the species most clearly distinguished based on sound properties, having a significantly higher pulse duration than M. zebra. When Amorim et al. focused specifically on M. sp. "zebra gold" and M. callainos, the two species for which they had the most data (most recorded males), they also found a significant difference in the number of pulses between the two species. In 1998, Lobel ("Possible Species Specific Courtship Sounds by Two Sympatric Cichlid Fishes in Lake Malawi Africa." Environ. Biol. Fishes 52:443-452), according to Amorim et al., had previously shown statistically significant differences in pulse rates and durations for two Malawian cichlids and proposed that courtship sounds could play a role in mate choice and species recognition. However, as Amorim et al. point out, the two species in that study, Copadichromis conophoros and Tramitichromis cf. intermedius, are not closely related, certainly not to the extent that the three species of Maylandias studied here are.

FACT #12 cont

As the authors point out, while their current results are tantalizing it remains to be demonstrated whether cichlids females of these cichlids in a particular can actually differentiate among males based on these courtship calls as is the case for frogs and insects. Though Amorim et al. wisely choose to interpret their results conservatively, they suggest that courtship signals involving sensory modalities other than vision, including acoustic (sound) and possibly olfactory (smell) may well be involved in cichlid species recognition and mate choice, and may have contributed to cichlid speciation. These suggestions await experimental confirmation, but I won't be surprised when it is demonstrated that female cichlids can and do choose mates on the basis not just for color, but also sound and smell.

FACT #13

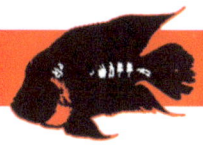

The most harmful natural enemies of cichlids are humans, pollution, large fish and birds.

In recent years, hundreds of fast- evolving fish species known as cichlids that swim in Africa's Great Lakes and Central / South America have gone extinct under the stresses of pollution and introduced predators. These fish also face the challenge of competing with evasive species like Tilapia which is farmed worldwide.

FACT #13 cont.

Not to mention the large predatory birds that often consume at least 3 large to medium sized cichlids a day when feeding their offspring.

Native overfishing in Central and South America also play a large role in the extinction of certain cichlid species.

FACT #14

Cichlids are protective and nurturing parents

Cichlids are very devoted parents. Both the male and female take care of the eggs during the incubation period. The male protects the nest against predators while the female moves her tail to mix water keeping the eggs aerated.

Cichlids are fearless when protecting their fry so be extra careful when keeping a community aquarium. Always look out for signs of courtship or pairing cichlids. A pair of cichlids can wreak havoc in your community tank. For further Evidence of these protective traits. Check-out this article from "The New York Times Magazine" by: Natalie Angier Titled- They're Smart, for Fish, And a Model of Diversity
By NATALIE ANGIER
Published: August 31, 1993

FACT #14

BERKELEY, Calif.— The date is a dud and both parties know it. Yet as long as they are stuck with each other for a time they make an effort to flirt. He lunges lazily toward her. She quivers gently in response. He flaps his tail against her. She flares her gills to show their provocative red undersides. He circles around, charges her again and tries to nip her, but now she's getting bored with the charade and moves away from him. Reacting likewise, he drifts off to the opposite end of the tank. For a few moments they are each lost in the inscrutable vastness of fish thought. And then it happens. The female opens her plump, sensuously carved lips into the widest, roundest, most perfect, least courteous gape of mouth that can be imagined: a fish yawn. "The female doesn't seem very interested, does she?" said Suzanne Henson, a student carrying out an experiment on the mating habits of cichlid (pronounced SICK-lid) fish. "She's not doing the sort of things you'd expect from a receptive female. She's not doing the slip motion, gliding her whole body along the body of the male."

FACT #14 cont

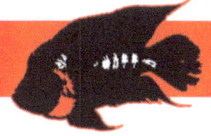

Sometimes, Ms. Henson said, when a female is put in a tank with a male, she becomes so excited that her genitals swell, and she immediately grows heavy with eggs. For his part, an interested male is a violent male, behaving toward his potential mate with an abusiveness that looks like grounds for criminal charges.

"Once a male bit a female so hard I jumped," said Ms. Henson. "I could hear the sound of the crunch." But not today, and not with these two slugs. Their disastrous date is finished, the experiment over, and each is returned to its proper tank.

Ms. Henson works in the laboratory of Dr. George W. Barlow of the University of California at Berkeley, a leading authority on the great and wildly diverse group of animals known as cichlid fish.

FACT #14 cont

She and others in the lab are studying the Midas cichlid, a beefy, square-jawed creature from Nicaragua that comes in two color schemes, zebra-striped or gold -- the last accounting for the species' name. Midas fish, like many other cichlids, are monogamous, and the researchers are seeking to understand the individual traits that inspire one Midas to choose another as its mate for life.

The question is part of a broader consideration of the sexual, social and feeding behaviors of cichlids, an extraordinary family of fish that many evolutionary biologists believe could help resolve the great puzzle of how species evolve and how diversity in nature arises from monotony. Assisting the new behavioral studies are molecular

FACT #14 cont

analyses of cichlid DNA, through which scientists are trying to determine relatedness between species and to map out the many twigs on the cichlid's dense and tangled family tree.

More than 1,000 species of cichlid fish live in the lakes and rivers of Africa, Madagascar, India and Latin America. They are a highly successful tribe, frequently dominating their environment through a blend of intelligence -- unusually high for a fish -- and elaborate rituals of parental care.

But what makes them so unusual is the number of species that often coexist in the same place. Over 500 different varieties of cichlids swim in Lake Malawi, in southeast Africa, while about 200 other species live in Lake Tanganyika, in Tanzania. Some species are bigger than goats, others could fit in a thimble. Some are thick and boxy, others lean and long. They are brown or turquoise or every shade of a neon rainbow painted on a single beast.

FACT #14 cont

And the cichlid's rate of speciation has been explosive. In Lake Victoria of East Africa, for example, 300 species of cichlids arose in less than 200,000 years, an evolutionary pace that no other animal group has rivaled.

Certainly, none of the other fish groups found in the three African lakes has undergone anything approaching the spectacular diversification managed by the cichlid family.

FACT #14 cont

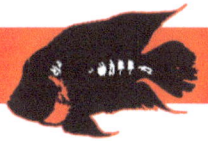

Scientists have long been captivated by cichlids, seeing in them a far greater opportunity to probe essential evolutionary patterns than was afforded by another famous family, Darwin's finches. Until recently, much of the research has relied on traditional taxonomic and observational approaches, tallying up species by studying fish anatomy, as well as by watching fish behavior.

Now biologists have added molecular analysis to their research, tracing cichlid lineages and cichlid radiations by studying the fish's DNA.

FACT #14 cont

In the current issue of the journal Trends in Ecology and Evolution, Dr. Axel Meyer, a molecular geneticist at the State University of New York at Stony Brook pulled together much of the recent molecular data on cichlid fish. The DNA work has confirmed previous results from the taxonomists that cichlids are monophyletic, that is, they all originate from a single ancestral fish that arose perhaps 120 million years ago,

when India, Africa and Latin America were one giant continent. Since the breakup of the continents, the founder fish that were carried off to different regions of the planet have gone their own ways, speciating wildly in all cases yet by very distinctive genetic mechanisms from one lake or river to another.

FACT #14 cont

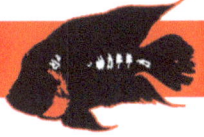

In some instances, species of cichlid fish that look and behave radically differently from one another turn out to be almost identical genetically.

For example, Dr. Meyer compared the DNA of 14 Lake Victoria cichlid species, choosing fish with radically divergent feeding behaviors: a snail eater, a cichlid that feeds on its fellow cichlids, a cichlid that eats only the eyes of other cichlids, another that exclusively sucks young cichlid fry out of the protective mouths of their parents. Yet despite the fishes' specialized appetites, their genes differ from one another by a mere two or three bases, or chemical subunits, out of the many hundreds of bases that constitute the genes examined. "This genetic invariance was a very big surprise to us," said Dr. Meyer. "There's more variation among human populations than I had among my fish." And humans, of course, are all members of the same species. Bizarre Hunting Strategies

The new work suggests that much of the success of the cichlid family could lie in its unusual degree of molecular flexibility, with minor differences in genes able to yield enormous disparities of comportment. And it is the cichlid's ability to specialize, scientists believe, that helps explain how so many species can live cheek by gill in the same body of water with each still managing to earn a living.

FACT #14 cont

If all cichlids were bottom grazers, for example, one species would likely outcompete the others into oblivion. But each cichlid has evolved its own hunting method, and each strategy seems more bizarre than the last. There is a cichlid that resembles a rotting fish and spends a lot of time floating as though dead; but when another fish approaches, thinking it has happened on an easy meal, the corpse springs to life and attacks the would-be scavenger.

A recent paper in the journal Science describes a newly discovered cichlid in Lake Tanganyika that has its head bent permanently to the left, an adaptation that enables its teeth to efficiently scrape a meal of scales off the right side of a passing fish's body. More improbable still, the researchers found a second type of cichlid that has evolved a head curving to the right, the better to shave scales from a prey fish's port side.

FACT #14 cont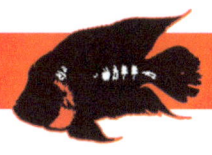

"There's always a new amazing story when you study cichlids," said Dr. Meyer. "The standard idea in ecology is that there are various niches waiting to be filled, and species arise to fill them. But cichlids seem to create their own niches."

Scientists believe that in a lake like Victoria or Tanganyika, the cichlids that originally founded the flocks were generalists, which then became specialists as competitive pressure increased.

Some scientists have suggested that cichlids have been able to evolve so many eating strategies by the grace of an unusual feature: They have two sets of jaws, one in their mouth, as the average fish does, and a second in their throat. With the throat jaws available to process food, the mouth jaws can be extremely flexible, evolving very specific methods for capturing food. "The idea here is that if you split the function into two jaws, there's less evolutionary constraint," said Dr. Melanie Stiassny, a cichlid expert at the American Museum of Natural History in New York. "In essence what you have here is a throat jaw that's a jack of all trades, and a mouth jaw that's a master of one."

FACT #14 cont

Variations in dining strategies, however, are not always the major distinguishing traits of cichlids. Reporting in the journal Nature last year, Dr. Meyer and Dr. Christian Sturmbauer, a co-worker, looked at the DNA of six cichlid species from Lake Tanganyika and found considerably more genetic variation than they had observed in Lake Victoria cichlids,

but in this case the predominant differences between the species were in their colors. And many cichlid biologists now believe that coloration holds another essential key to the fish family's story, for coloration often goes with sexuality and mating preferences, among the more potent driving forces in evolution. "A Fish Called Wanda"

FACT #14 cont

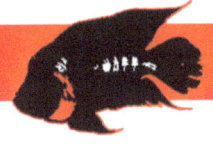

Cichlids have always been popular fish among home aquarium hobbyists; Wanda in the movie "A Fish Called Wanda" was a South American cichlid. Fish keepers claim cichlids are so bright, they recognize individual humans, but people are especially taken with the fish's courtship and fry-rearing practices. Most fish lay eggs and abandon them, or the father may remain to watch the eggs until they hatch. But among cichlids, both parents often engage in protracted parental care. They brood their eggs in their mouths, and even after the fry are born, they protect the little fish by taking them back into the safety of their mouths when predators approach. "They'll suck the fry back in as though they're sucking in strands of spaghetti," said Dr. Barlow of the University of California at Berkeley.

The habit of mouth brooding has led to a few outstanding features on male cichlids. Because predatory pressure in a cichlid's habitat can be extreme, many females, after laying their eggs, frantically turn around and begin scooping them into their mouths before the eggs have been fertilized. Males have adapted to this by evolving bright spots on their rear fins that strongly resemble eggs. When the female is sucking in her eggs, the male gives his rear fin a shake, she tries to take the dummy eggs into her mouth, and -- whoosh! -- the male releases a stream of semen into the female's mouth that then fertilizes the eggs.

In some species, both parents also feed their fry with their own flesh, allowing the young fish to nibble at the scales and nutritious mucus cells on the surface of their bodies. "The parent is a big breast is what it amounts to," said Dr. Barlow.

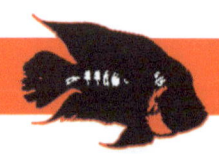

FACT #14 cont

Given the high investment that parents make in their young and in each other, scientists propose, cichlids must have ways of selecting worthy partners. Fish are visually oriented, so it is likely that they pick mates based on cues of color. Dr. Meyer suggests that sexually selected traits like color may undergo far more rapid divergence than would traits that affect an animal's ability to survive, and hence could partly explain the explosive evolution of cichlids.

In experiments with the Midas cichlids, Dr. Barlow and his co-workers are trying to tease out the details of mate preference. They have learned that although only about 8 percent of the species develop a gold coat, both other gold's and the dull zebra-stripers prefer a mate of gold when given the choice.

That could be because the gold's look more threatening. Cichlids must often fight off outsiders when rearing their brood, and so toughness in a mate is highly valued. Through their detailed matchmaking trials, the scientists have learned that mate choice proceeds in two steps. First, the female finds a male who appeals to her, for reasons that the scientists have yet to glean. But once the female has demonstrated a liking for the male, he will start exerting his own choosiness by behaving extremely aggressively toward her.

FACT #14 cont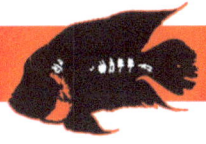

"He's testing the female to see if she's aggressive enough," said Dr. Barlow. "She's got to threaten him back in the right way if he's going to accept her." Once the male has determined that the female is tough enough, he will mate with her and treat her gently ever thereafter.

The odds of a male and female cichlid sharing just the right color and chemistry are slim, which is why so many Midas encounters end in fish ennui and a giant fish yawn.

FACT #15

Cichlids can adapt faster and better than any species of fish.

Cichlids can adapt to the changes in their environment faster than any other species of fish in the world. Therefore, fish species are meticulously studied by researchers quite often. I (fishlaw1) have studied the behavior and abilities of these fish for a very long time and still find it remarkable how quickly and completely they are able to adjust and adapt to their environment almost seamlessly.

BONUS FISH FACTS

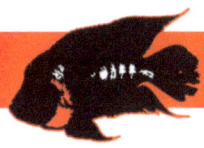

1.) Did you know Skip was the first fish keeper to start and name an Aquatic kennel? "Real Hard Cichlids Aquatic kennels"

2.) Did you know that like humans' fish have five senses? These senses are utilized to assist in acquiring food (prey), to defend against predators and in some cases for schooling with others of their own species.

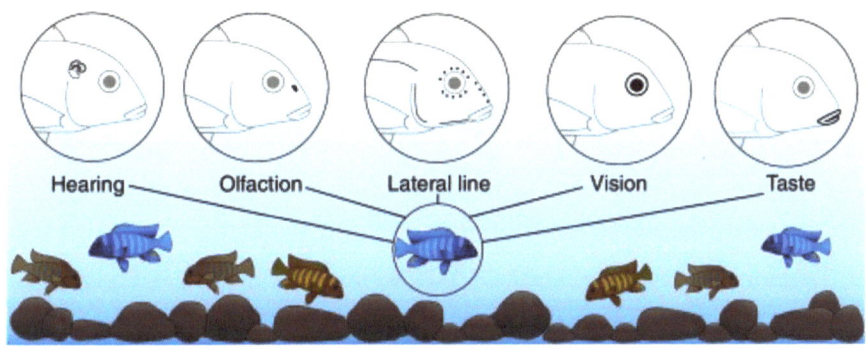

Let's examine the senses.

Sight- The eyes of a fish are not much different than that of a human; however, fish lack true eyelids, because their eyes are under water always, thus no need for eyelids. Also, some fish have better vision than their counterparts, others only can see light and dark and lastly can see in color. (A cool fact)!

Smell- Fish have nostrils called nares which are located on the snout above their mouths. Under the skin just below the nares openings are small sacs which contain smell receptors, the water carrying scent moves through their sacs. The sacs are connected to by the brain nerves, allowing the fish to smell and like sharks who have an extremely acute sense of smell so does fish.

46.

BONUS FISH FACTS

Taste- Fish can taste with their snout, mouth, tongue and throat. A fish's tongue has taste buds just like us; however, they are unable to retract their tongue. Further the tongue of a fish can only move when the lower jaw moves. The species Walleye have taste buds located on their heads, as well as, in their mouths. Additionally, they can taste lures or bait by bumping into them with their face. Catfish have whiskers called barbels, loaded with taste buds. They use their whiskers to feel around in the mud and when they find something tasty they stop and bite it!

Hearing- Fish have two ways they can hear; via otoliths or a lateral line. Otoliths are inner ear bones in a fish skull. Tiny hairs called cilia are located on the otolith which can be stimulated by the fish's brain. Some fish have heightened sense of hearing due to close-proximity of swim bladder to the otolith.

Feeling- Fish have another sensory organ called the (lateral line), which is a sense organ of microscopic pores used to detect movement and vibration in surrounding water. The lateral line consists of sensory receptors called neuromasts. When the cilia in the neuromasts vibrate, the fish can feel and detect water pressure (depth), prey and predators' movement.

BONUS FISH FACTS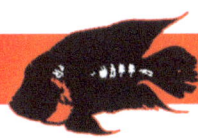

3.) Did you know Skip was the first fish keeper to introduce terms like bloodlines, lineage and pedigrees to the Central and South American Cichlids keepers?

4.) Did you know Skip was the first hobbyist to present a physical pedigree certificate for cichlids on the world – wide web?

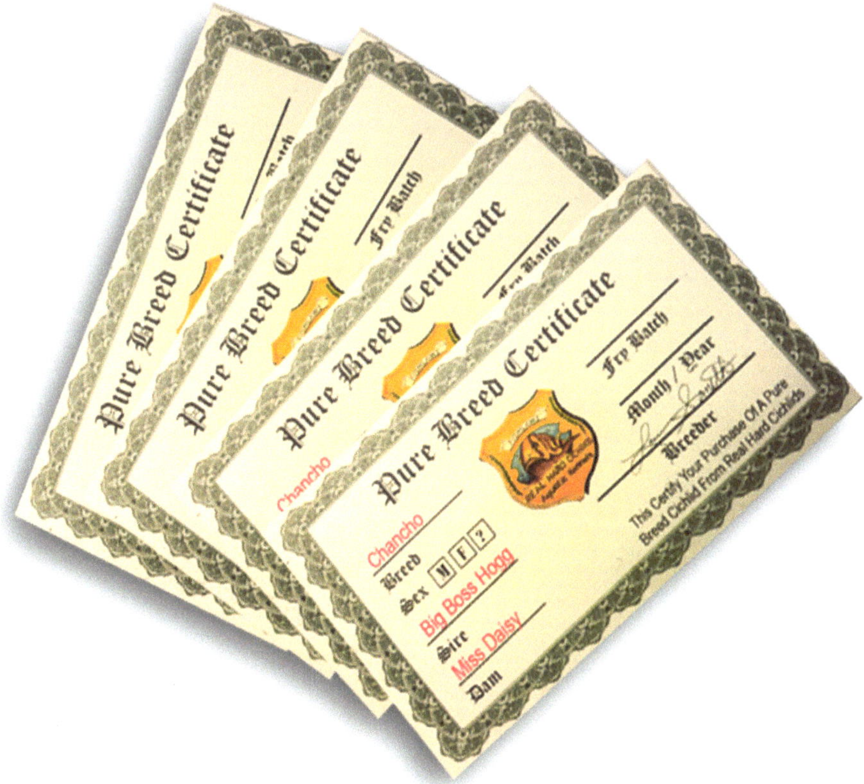

5.) Did you know Skip has one of the oldest known cichlid bloodline in the world; the Pyro Trimac Cichlid which spans over two decades.

SHOW ME THE FISH FACTS

Use the following pages to write your notes,
and be on your way to having an insightful conversation with fellow hobbyist.

SHOW ME THE FISH FACTS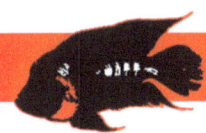

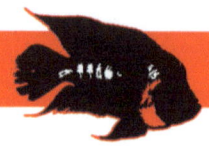

SHOW ME THE FISH FACTS

SHOW ME THE FISH FACTS

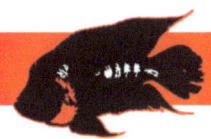

Resources

RightsLinks: Copyright Clearance Center

Title: Sensory modalities in cichlid fish behavior Chart

Author: Daniel Escobar-Camacho, Karen L. Carleton

Publication: Current Opinion in Behavioral Sciences

Publisher: Elservier

Date: December 2015

The "New York Times Magazine Article" by: Natalie Angier

Titled – They're Smart, for Fish, And a Model of Diversity

Published: August 31, 1993

Art Director: Mr. William Kato Harrs of Cre8tive Conceptions

Photo Resources: Shutter Stock

Photo Resources: Istock

Photo Resources: Juan E. Olivo

Photo Resources: Sean Johnson

Photo Resources: Kato Harris

www.ingramcontent.com/pod-product-compliance
Lightning Source LLC
Chambersburg PA
CBHW042333150426
43194CB00001B/43